Pieces of Humanity

Skylar J Wynter

DEDICATION

For

Kate and Richard

You helped me with the pieces

Be prepared for the skin to be peeled back with this read, exposing the flesh and barebones of the complex soul through a blend of flash fiction, short stories, and poetry. Cutting straight to the chase with raw words that pack a punch, this read goes straight to the heart of the taboo. Depression, suicide, and euthanasia are explored here with no barriers, but the author perfectly balances hard-hitting themes with soft tones of family, love, and ultimately freedom, to make choices in death just as we expect to make choices in life. I'm always drawn to literary work that does not shy away from confronting realities and Pieces of Humanity does not disappoint. An exceptional debut collection from Skylar J Wynter.

Kelly Van Nelson, Author and Poet.

AUTHORS NOTE

This book is the result of a series of events that broke me into a million pieces. I had a choice: let the pieces disappear into the ether, or try and collect them up, make sense of them and hopefully put them back together. Even in my darkest moments, when the pain of existing and the sense of being alone, disjointed, weird, out of step, was bigger than what I could hold in, a tiny tether of self-preservation, a whisper of belief that if I held on long enough I could find my way back to connection with self and then others, remained.

The universe colluded and conspired and after a time gifted me with two people; Kate Negoscue and Richard Magtengaard, who have made it their life's work to understand trauma; its effects and how to treat it, and in turn, with infinite compassion create safe spaces where the traumatised can be treated, can come to understand both the physiological and emotional changes that trauma brings and begin their journey of compassion for self, collecting up the pieces and finding acceptance in a new way of being.

I have always been my own worst critic. I still am but it is tempered and buffered by a gentleness that was born of the understanding these two incredible people knew I needed to have as an intrinsic first step in the process of healing. I am changed by this experience. I have lost pieces and gained new ones, but now I understand; the puzzle that is me, the puzzle of each of us, is ever changing. If we embrace this changing out of pieces, then we embrace what it is to be human. Acceptance if you like, that brings an element of peace and hope even when the critic is screaming blue murder.

At some point, I had the realisation that this strange disconnected experience I was living, this reality where what I was feeling, thinking, living on the inside was the complete opposite to what I was presenting to the world in an effort to look and behave normally, was a huge part of why I felt so alone, so disconnected. What if everyone is living this way? I thought. What if I began living life through the lens that every stranger I met or passed in the street, friend or family member, had the same gap between their external and internal reality? Suddenly I felt less alone. Suddenly I was not the only one who had a story beneath the surface. Suddenly when I held this thought in my head when going through the motions of living, I began to really get interested about what was going on for others. What was their story? What was driving them? Even though I thought I knew this person, did I really? Suddenly instead of feeling angry and disconnected and resentful that the person talking to me had no idea who I was and what was going on for me, I was wanting to know about them. I began to feel connected. It wasn't that I became the world's greatest interrogator or nosy parker imploring people to share their secrets. No, I'd just found a new piece. I began interacting with the belief that whatever exchange I was sharing, things are never as they seem. Never.

I had conversations I never thought I would have. Stories and poems I never thought I could write were written, ideas and concepts and perspectives I'd not been able to see before arrived on the pages of my notebook and I found that by assuming everyone had a hidden life beneath their surface compassion naturally arose, and judgement diminished. A rigid opinion about any given topic felt arrogant. I was suddenly willing to ask, What do you think? and consider the answer not from my own internal reality but from theirs. I was interested in the why and how of their perspective rather than the right or wrong of it. The story not the ending.

With the trauma came many gifts and it is no flippant remark when I say I am grateful for those and the many lessons I received. Some of them I hated. They sucked.

They were painful and debilitating. Some were and continue to be a joy. Without all of them collectively - there would be no book. New friendships have been forged, new experiences had, and all have come together to land me here and now.

My hope for the stories and poems within the pages of this book is that they will impart no lectures, no instructions on how to live life, embrace death or anything in-between, they are simply works of fiction bringing into focus the possibility of a variety of human moments, thoughts and perspectives laying beneath the surface of any one of us.

Hopefully, like I did, you will feel less alone knowing that we all have a gap, and in recognising it, compassion, hope and validation can come to the fore in the moments we share. Pieces shared and received will fill the gaps to complete the biggest puzzle of all – humanity.

CONTENTS

EXPERIENCE………....................1

QUIET CORRUPTION…………...…...2

SO ANNOYING…………………….…5

SURVIVAL………………………....11

MONSTER…………………………...12

WASTED……………………….…..21

DAMAGED GOODS …………….…..24

FRAGILITY……………………….26

CHANGES……………………….27

NOT READY……………………30

ALONE………………………….…33

OBSESSION………………….…..35

DESPAIR……………………….....39

TOO LATE……………………40

REFLECT………………………43

PROOF OF LIFE……………………...44

FORTUITOUS............................48

MASTERS OF DISGUISE..............54

INSANITY..................................56

WHY NOT?................................57

SHAME....................................60

IMPACT...................................61

CLICHÉ...................................65

ALREADY ENOUGH....................70

URBAN HAIKU..........................74

RETREAT.................................76

Q AND NO A.............................80

DILLIGAF................................84

CHOOSE..................................89

NOT YOUR FAULT....................90

BLURRED LINES.......................93

SHADES OF GREY.....................96

A PROPER JOB........................102

RAW....................................104

BOUNDARIES……………………………..108

THE HUMANE THING…………………110

EYES UP………………………………...116

HEART OF GLASS……………………..119

ACCEPT…………………………..…...121

SMILE AT THE PARTY………………..122

ALL I NEEDED TO KNOW……………..127

ENTIRELY PAINLESS…………………..131

OKAY…………………………………..134

HOMEWARD BOUND…………………150

PIECES OF HUMANITY………………..151

RAW EMOTION FELT

IS THE EXPERIENCE

OF BEING HUMAN

QUIET CORRUPTION

Quiet quiet calm

Talking talking talking

Questions answers

Questions ANSWERS

QUESTIONS ANSWERS

OVERWHELM

SNAP!

Shouting shrieking screaming

Swearing cursing hating

Ears heart doors

Ringing pounding slamming

Guilt despair devastation

Misery loss desolation

Mind body person

Altered broken fading

Mouth throat chest

Dry tight heaving

Mother child husband

Trying crying pleading

Overwrought bewildered shaking

Self-loathing overtaking

What madness is this?

Neither sought nor invited

An unwelcome guest

Arriving without warning

Appearing coming going spoiling

A cunning assailant

Engulfing destroying

Wreaking havoc laying waste

Leaving guilt and heartbreak

In its wake

Exhausted surrender

Breath in

Breath out

Regroup watch wait

Uneasy

Sweat drenched queasy

Dreading fearing despising

The vicious eruption

Soul-destroying corruption

Of the quiet, quiet calm

SO ANNOYING

My daughter's footsteps bruise the floorboards as she hurricanes up the hallway to her room.

"You're so annoying. I fucking hate you," her parting shot.

I am broken, crushed; feeling every measure of hopeless. The weight of it sits tingling between throat and chest trapping a sob and oxygen beneath its crush.

How have I, once loved beyond measure, once the goddess of my daughter's world, once so connected by the uncontrived relationship of nurturing mother and nurtured child, now be so wrong, so hated, so despised?

It was the sneer that did it this time. A bunching of muscles twisting her usually sweet features into a look no mother wants to see. Her eyes, full of mocking challenge (or was it hate) and her lips curved as though her mouth contained something disgusting that needed to be spat out.

Does every mother feel she has more lives than a cat when eventually signs of life begin to return, just barely, after every emotional slaying at the hands of their child? Or is that just me? How many lives do I have left, I wonder? How can my chest feel the hollowness of despair and, at the same time, the tightness of being full of an emotion so big I can't name it?

I stare, unseeing, at the space she has just stormed from, wanting to weep freely, sob like a baby and have her run back to comfort me. See her eyes, full of concern that she has hurt me so cruelly. What I would do to see her features soften with love, a reflection of genuine remorse; hear some words of apology that echo with transparency and truth.

But my tears remain trapped with the sob and I remind myself it is I who am the adult. I must remain calm: hold the boundary, remain unphased, carry on with my day as though I have not, in fact, had my heart torn from my body or my lungs rendered useless from crush injuries. Wait for another day, time or place when she is calm, to talk with her about good and bad choices, and how they will earn or lose her privileges. I must know exactly the moment to stop the conversation, so it doesn't escalate once more, and further hurt can remain unspoken.

She has cut me so deeply, her words of hate stripping away all the protective layers I constructed to become an adult, that now all that is left is the child I once was. I feel diminished. Tiny. Bewildered. A terror, akin to what you feel the first time you get lost as a child, starts to creep over my skin. That horror that awakens deep in your psyche, as your four-year-old eyes look up to see the hem of the skirt you have tugged on to get mother's attention does not, in fact, wear your mother's face, is welling and growing and filling me so I feel sure it will have no option but to shred me from the inside out.

My hands have been white-knuckling the kitchen bench and I force myself to relax my grip, stretching out my fingers and turning each hand, palm upwards so I can read the words *Breathe* and *This Too Will Pass* inked prettily on each wrist.

My husband hates tattoos. Was it selfish of me to get them anyway? To take the time and money to do something just for me? It didn't feel like it; the burning pain of the thin, soft skin being more like a penance than a rebellion. Having them done serves to remind me not only of how to survive such pain-filled moments, but also that I would no longer have a self to be selfish about if I concerned myself more with pleasing his personal tastes than my own.

I hear her footsteps pounding back up the hallway and busy myself with cleaning the stovetop that is already sparkling; anything, so she doesn't see the child I have momentarily become.

"Happy now?"

I don't have to turn to know the sneer is still plastered on her face. Her voice is laden with it. I don't trust myself to reply.

"Yeah, that's what I thought. You're such a fucked-up bitch. You don't even care what I look like, you just want to control me. I fucking hate you, and the things you wear are bloody ugly. Every time you go out, I'm embarrassed, but I don't tell you your clothes suck, so why don't you just leave me the fuck alone to wear what I want?"

I still don't answer.

"Are you seriously going to let her speak to you like that?" My son's voice sounds out of his room.

"Shut the fuck up," she screams back. "You're such an arsehole."

"And you're a stupid dumb bitch," is his reply.

I look down at my wrists again.

"God, you're so annoying. I'm going to Charlie's."

"No, you're..." I begin

"Shut up. You can't stop me." And she's gone.

She's right. I can't stop her. And I can't stop myself as the tears and the sobs finally break through. I lower myself to the kitchen floor and give in to the thing that has robbed me of being the mother I wanted to be.

SURVIVAL

Breathe in. Breathe out.

Suppress. Refrain. Control. Don't shout.

Attend to tasks with love devout.

Provide. Surrender. Tears in. Smiles out.

Let those around you never construe

An image of you

You can't undo.

MONSTER

Exhaustion floods my body, drowning my spirit but heightening my senses so every emotion is a bloated, unmanageable exaggeration of itself. Nerve endings lie so close to my surface that breathing is movement enough to expose them.

Sleep is the only activity that offers comfort, and fantasies of a more permanent rest fray the fabric of whatever is holding me together. I feel myself becoming threadbare; not knitted together enough to contain, restrain or maintain my fucked-up life. Imagine waking up with the dry horrors to the power of ten, and that is one-hundredth of the thirst I have for death.

But I can't do it. A blatant example of me choosing not to help myself. I couldn't bear to leave life as I live it; hating myself, despising my actions and the hurt it will cause my family, leaving them to think they weren't enough to keep me here.

My pain is a fucking vicious, piece-of-shit monster. It grows more immense by the day, gorging and sapping life from every vibrating atom. It's always hungry, demanding sustenance, so I try to starve it. Give it nothing that fosters growth or fleshes out the hollowness it's creating. I visualise shrinking it to a size I can contain and manage, but it has ways of backing me into corners so tight there's no option but to succumb. Empty of hope or any other good thing, I am left feeling like sweet fuck all. Smaller than sweet fuck all, but not small or fuck all enough to get out of that corner.

I crave a monster-less space: quiet, safe, peaceful, painless.

This monster has devoured so much of me, I don't know or recognise what's left. It hunts down every tiny piece, no matter how long forgott and feasts.

I am submerged in a kind of hell that tortures me nearly to death, before serving up a random, monster-free moment that gets me higher than stoned on hope, that it's gone for good.

There are people that sit in safe spheres and ask me to tell them my story. They think the retelling will somehow purge it once and for all from the dark crevices of my mind and body. Instead, it just feeds that fucking cunt of a monster and he stuffs himself full to bursting with all the dredged-up trauma and pain.

Afterwards, its poison spews out like a geyser over friends, family, strangers in the wrong place at the wrong time. I have zero filters; the bastard has gorged on those too. In the days following, I wake filled with shame, self-loathing smothering me like a too-heavy blanket, and the monster feeds again. He isn't choosy with his meals.

I know another like me, but not at all like me, who understands, gets the whole wanting nothing but sleep, thing.

Understands that all-consuming anguish of needing the world to stop, but not wanting to be the arsehole that stops it. Passive suicidal thoughts, she calls it.

She tells me she has a monster as well. A demon who whispers foul bullshit into her ears. She lives in a state of high alert; the world a dangerous place. I've seen her go from zip to panicked out of her fucking mind in less than a moment if she hears a siren or someone honks a horn in her vicinity. Full-blown bloody dangerous driver crazy takes over, leaving her with a stomach full of bile she is too scared to pull over and heave up in case the fear of getting back on the road keeps her at its edge, frozen and helpless. I sat in a room with her once, before I understood what she was living with, and watched the tired, hopeless tears roll down her face as she tried to explain, to whoever the fuck else was there, what was going on with her. None of us really tried to get it and I feel like a real shit when I think on it. How she faces the world every day without drugs is beyond me. Strangers, friends, family, have little insight into her inner catastrophic storm. All you see on the outside is a good-looking chick with her shit together. A bloody master of disguise blending in, so no-one suspects the craziness beneath.

Her vicious monster gorges on fear, self-loathing and self-criticism. It chants abuse straight into the guilt centres of her brain any time she allows herself a slice of cake or bar of chocolate. It feasts on the disgust she feels and tears she sheds, hiding in her wardrobe. It screams lies, undermining and vicious, into her mind until she believes she's a bad mum, shit at controlling her anxiety, a waste of oxygen. Feeling like a failure nearly every fucking moment of every fucking day is her norm.

Shocked the hell out of me to hear that stuff, but hearing it helped me feel not quite so alone.

She knows things I have never known; her current state of being, only new. Another past way of experiencing life has her believing that compassion and validation can make all the difference, while judgement and processes within the system hold us captive in obtuse cavities we can't possibly negotiate our way out of.

I get pretty bent out of shape about the millions of dollars spent on systems that are designed to make the users fail, the frustration playing an endless loop in my brain.

It's a sick joke when sociologists get funding to study ancient cultures under the premise of uncovering clues as to how we got to where we are now. No stone is left unturned in the quest to understand past human adaptation to everchanging environments. Do individuals in the present, and how we try and adapt to environmental stresses, pique such interest? Only on social experiment reality TV, it seems to me. One thing is certain: any conclusions drawn on human behaviour, be it ancient or present, are interpretations only, made by third parties who can only guess at the realities of others. These conclusions become judgements, which become fodder for problem-solving solutions. Any needy soul with access to these solutions who fails to adapt and reform is subjected to the judgement that started it all.

Trust me, I know I'm here because of my fucked-up choices. Knowing this; the shame, the self-loathing, the completely useless worthlessness of me; sabotages any efforts to fix myself. I can't be fixed. I can't change. And you can't stop judging me. You can't stop sneering when you look at my tattooed body, shaved head, or house on the dodgy side of town.

She says I'm the strongest person she knows and notices me making a daily choice to keep living. To keep searching for that which will fix un-fixable me; a pain-stealing elixir. Known side effects: the erasure of neural highways deeply imprinted under the weight of semi-trailers loaded up with all the behavioural patterns and thoughts that keep me from living a better life.

I don't need fixing; her opinion, not mine. I need to be taken care of for a while so I can rest, be cradled like I wasn't as a child, have all my needs met in a safe space until my nervous system is soothed and I no longer feel under threat. Only then will my brain be able to learn new things, new ways of being that are rooted in rational thought, not adrenaline-filled reaction.

The Monster has a great fucking laugh over that. Tells me I deserve no love, no kindness, no nurturing. Tells me I am less than nothing, not worth even the glance of passers-by. I give in, injecting Valium straight into the vein to shut the fucker up. I will fall into a sleep, deep enough to silence his bullshit snickering and abuse. If no-one will let me legally, peacefully, drift away into endless sleep, I will do what I can to grant myself a few hours of unconsciousness. You see? I am not searching for the high of a junkie, I am searching for a reprieve because I'm fucking exhausted.

I'll drift off, tears of defeat sliding uselessly down my cheeks and what's left of my heart and soul, wretchedly craving the day I can choose permanent slumber over a few shitty hours. Death, at a time of my own choosing, less traumatic and lonely than suicide, legalised by those who act from selflessness and compassion instead of judgement and disdain.

Do they realise – the judgers and haters – that they are the personification of this monster on my back?

WASTED

Invisible girl cries

when size ten doesn't fit

Daily sustenance, fresh air,

till she's shrunk quite a bit

Popular girl wishes

she fit into size six

Skip food, chew gum

recipe for a quick fix

Boy hits puberty,

testosterone floods his being

He's horrified, devastated

at the changes happening

Repulsed, disgusted,

hating the body, he sees

Starves himself, desperate,

to feel more like she, than he

Wants to be waif-like,

wear the gorgeous little jeans

He sees on the pages

of teen magazines

Busy, tired mum,

husband starts to stray

If she can just get thin enough,

he'll throw plaything away

Girl, boy, mum,

sister, brother, friend

If they're thinner, taller, blonder

from self-loathing they'll ascend

Looking in their mirrors,

Despising what is naked

Starved of self-love, self-worth and food,

Leaves souls and bodies wasted

DAMAGED GOODS

New places scare the shit out of me. What can I say?
I am damaged goods. Cray-cray. A bit odd. Whatever. At
nineteen I have already seen too much, suffered too many
traumas to bore you with, and created a life that could only
be described as a desert. A barren place, with hardly any
proof of life aside from the beating of my own terrified
heart, and measurable thoughts of managing past and pre-
sent, while sparing no time or energy to dwell on a future.

A single list dictates my life. To stray from the list is
not an option. Though not overly concerned with planning
a future, staying alive seems inherent, and besides, plan-
ning to die is still future-planning in my view, but
something has happened. I am left with no choice. A co-
nundrum. My stampeding heart beats double-time and my
brain churns with thoughts that are no longer measurable.
They are spewing out of unused places, causing long-

forgotten neurons to misfire and search for the correct routes – which once were major highways, but are now less than ant trails – across and through my list-managed brain. I try to quell them. Time for thinking is not on the agenda. My body feels rigid with the effort. My eyes, normally either staring or closed, are flicking about wildly. The thoughts will not be quelled.

I do the only thing that I can: I surrender.

My bed comes to a standstill. Brakes on wheels are clamped. My eyes register that this room is no different from the last. A new place, but the same as the old. My heart slows, my eyes go back to staring, and I continue on with following the list. *Eat* comes after *recite list*. A few minutes late, due to my relocation, a nurse moves into view and attaches a bag containing my liquid breakfast to the tube that tracks a path through my nasal cavity and down the back of my throat.

Like I said. Damaged goods.

FRAGILITY

Falling, falling, crash

Broken pieces of me lie

Exposed, vulnerable

Reaching, reaching, catch

My sharp edges cut you deep

Leaving you ragged

CHANGES

Tremendous booms sound out across the sky. Showers of colour pop and explode, making my granddaughter, Lucy, squeal. Delight or terror, I can't be sure until I look down, see her baby hands clapping and chubby cheeks bunched into a smile.

It's all done with lights and sound now. The last time I felt the boom of fireworks in my body was 2018. That was fifty years ago. The coloured sparks would waterfall down over the Swan River while our parents sat on its banks, enjoying a Christmas Eve drink and platters of food with friends. We children frolicked and played in its muddy water. The evening would stretch out for hours, but for us, it was gone in a flash.

Now we stay home; safer that way. We watch computer-generated images of fireworks on a screen that covers an entire wall, making the experience seem real enough, but without the pollution.

Afterwards, Lucy on my knee, we sing carols. The words have been changed to ensure no-one is offended. The decorated tree in the corner is no longer called a Christmas tree – I forget why.

So many things are different. A changed world. At ninety I have experienced a variety of Christmas Eves and unwrapped countless gifts. As a child, I would delight in the bathing suit or sugary treat hidden within the bright wrappings. With the passing of time the gifts became bigger, mass-produced items, that cost a lot and broke quickly.

My wandering thoughts are interrupted as Lucy scrambles down from my knee. With the singing over, the moment she has been waiting for all evening has arrived. Tearing the paper off her midnight gift, she pulls out a soft, colourful ball my daughter has crocheted. Landfill is full and life has come full circle. People delight in hand made gifts and the bounty of their veggie patch once more.

I am celebrating my last Christmas, filled less with excitement than pain. Despite all the changes over the years, a cure for what savagely gnaws away at my body has not been found. In three days, I will lay in my soft bed, surrounded by family. They will smile, hold my hand and reminisce about my life. There will be laughter and wine and home-made nibbles, much like the Christmas Eves of my childhood. Relief, rather than tears, will flow around the room as I drift peacefully away from my pain. Relief that the world has changed enough to allow me the choice to go quietly, painlessly, surrounded by love.

That, I think, is the popular consensus.

NOT READY

Synesthesia: A perceptual phenomenon in which stimulation of one sensory or cognitive pathway leads to automatic, involuntary experiences in another.

Bewilderment; a feeling of being perplexed and confused, is no stranger to me. It tastes as it sounds, a multitude of flavours confusing the buds on my tongue and leaving me unable to describe it at all. I see numbers as colours, hear colours as sounds and see letters as people with specific clothes and personalities. Black is a note low and sombre; yellow, high and tinkling. *I* is a skinny man walking on stilts, with yellow flared pants, who picks his nose.

My life is a cacophony of visual, auditory, tactile and taste overload. *Your* senses process millions of pieces of information a day; *mine* multiply them out like some quantum calculation there is as yet no formula for.

The world is not ready for me. It's not equipped to understand, let alone help.

I live alone, don't go out. Thick curtains block my windows. I have no smartphone, no TV; anything I wanted to watch would fail to have meaning once my senses processed the information into an unsolvable maze. As a child, I was labelled Autistic. I'm not. I just couldn't stand the noise, the tastes, the sounds of life. Since then I have been poked, prodded, tested, observed and diagnosed with any number of rare disorders, behavioural conditions and personality syndromes. With every new label came a new medication to soften its symptoms.

Wrong labels. Wrong medications.

The world is not ready for me. I cannot be in it. I will remain in this bubble until I die; not a life at all, sleep the only remedy. An induced coma until research catches up and a cure can be found. *Too costly*, I was told by a doctor who thought I was joking when I suggested it. Costly tastes like lemons and smells like old socks so I started drooling and choking. He panicked thinking I was having a fit and failed to connect the dots, see my bigger picture. I asked for a more permanent fix and was put on suicide watch. All the letters that spell suicide have funny personalities, wear top hats and bow ties, and behave badly, so I laughed when I saw it written down in his notes. A psychotropic drug was prescribed, but nothing I could use to attain permanent sleep.

The world is not ready to offer me that.

Live on I must. With no life at all.

ALONE

Solitary

Finite

Singular

One

Terms of measurement

Not of emotion

As one I am separate

Isolated, frozen

Part of two

But I not we

Part of three

The third wheel is me

Part of a team

Subbed off not on

Part of a crowd

Identity gone

Empty

Vacuous

Devoid

Alone

Terms of emotion

Measurement unknown

OBSESSION

She's at it again. My heart sinks. I swaddle my head tight within my pillow, compressing my cheeks so the flesh is forced downwards to wrinkle and bunch at my jaw; my jowls will not be thanking me in years to come.

Night after night I have assumed this position in an attempt to mute the incessant buzzing, vibrating through the adjacent wall of the apartment next door. The noise, now begun, will continue intermittently for several hours; the woman next door has obsessive needs that must be met. I don't wish to imagine the degradation of the delicate pink flesh that suffers nightly under the humming, oscillating probe in her hand, but images of this hidden, soft place (grazed, bloody and swollen beyond any capability to endure further traffic) come anyway.

I loosen my grip on my pillow, regretting it instantly. The low buzzing has been joined by another sound, not unexpected, but less easy to drown out: haunting moans, edged with a fragility that validate my conclusions on the condition of the flesh she seems so bent on destroying, in search of satiating her misunderstood needs.

I have painstakingly witnessed her condition worsen in recent weeks and know she needs to possess a will of iron to beat it before it beats her. I know if I attempt to silence her by tapping on the wall, the interruption will make things worse, take her back to the start.

A sob, caught and held half-way between chest and throat before exploding outwards in a raw bark, comes through the wall, boring into my ear canals and tearing through my heart. Silence follows and I start to count. It is only a matter of time and she will have no choice but to begin again. Two-hundred-and-sixty-three seconds; twenty-three seconds longer than last time, which was thirteen seconds longer than the time before. She is trying to get the upper hand; get control over the uncontrollable.

Tears prick at my eyes as I think of this morning when I left for work. She had been fumbling the lock on her apartment door with hands red raw, I knew, within her sterile gloves. Filled with compassion, I'd raised my eyes in the hope of meeting hers and conveying something. Not pity, but something that would help. The sight of her abused mouth; lips swollen, covered in sores and rubbed raw from the obsessive use of her electric toothbrush night after night, broke something I had not previously known existed, deep in my soul.

I am a useless observer, watching a disorder not wholly understood, rip apart her life as she strips her delicate mouth with the compulsive, repetitive scrubbing required to quell her all-consuming panic that she missed a spot with her first, second or tenth attempt.

Hers is the mouth I have dreamt of kissing my whole life, but never will; the unavoidable germs inhabiting mine, presenting an insurmountable barrier to me ever being more than a witness; distant and silent to her pain

and suffering.

DESPAIR

A

single tear

rolls down my cheek

The grief behind it is not unique

Not a strange, uncommon, or unknown thing

Not unusual, or special, but soul-destroying

I am all alone and unable to care

Filled with low-grade,

chronic, silent

despair

TOO LATE

I cower:

    In the hall

    Under the bed

    Against the wall

I cover:

    The bruises, black

    My frightened child

    My abuser's tracks

I lie:

    For my own sake

    No-one can know

    Reputation to fake

I smother:

    Cries of pain

    Paralysing fear

    Tears of shame

I escape:

> To another place
>
> In mind not body
>
> Where all are safe

I vow:

> To stop the pain
>
> Despite the fear
>
> I cannot remain

Too late:

> The mood misread
>
> Before I could run
>
> Now I am dead

REFLECT

REFLECT ON WHAT IS

QUESTION WHAT CAN BE

OPEN YOUR MIND AND EYES

AND BE WILLING TO SEE

PROOF OF LIFE

Parenthood envisioned

With your rapid heartbeat

Had your life mapped out

Expected joy, not grief

Proof of life beats rhythm

Keeping time with my own

Nausea stopped along with your heart

We were gutted, bereft, alone

D and C scraped me clean

Cluster of cells, not human being

Apparently

Thirteen weeks, another heart

Beat strong inside my womb

Specks of blood I denied

Brought a crushing sense of doom

D and C scraped me clean

Cluster of cells, not human being

Apparently

Eyelids, nose, arms and legs

You stayed within until

At sixteen weeks I felt first pains

You left against my will

Induced contractions pushed you free

Not cluster of cells nor human being

Apparently

Not surviving twenty weeks

There's no certificate of life or death

I can get one of recognition though

By applying on the internet

Heartbeat within, proof of being

Until it's without means nothing it seems

Unbelievably

We tried again, tested the fates

Hoped *this* time you'd come into being

Twenty weeks; *all good*, we thought

Then nightmare corrupted the dream

Pain and suffering infinite

As from my body, you did slip

Unbelievably

Arrival was not registered

Because you were born dead

No birth or death certificate

Just a stillborn one instead

Life *and* death only registered

If it happens *outside* my uterus

Unbelievably

The shock, the grief and pain of loss

is not changed by its location

Healing is assisted though

With recognition and validation

Proof of life begins with a heart

Let's acknowledge where it starts

Unforgettably

FORTUITOUS

They'd arrived late. Too late for everything but the sunset today. The woman, along with the dozens of other tourists sharing wine and laughter in the designated viewing area, was looking forward to it, although the evening breeze off the desert set a chill in her.

"Surely you're not cold?" The woman's husband had noticed the goosebumps, felt the involuntary shiver against his chest.

"A bit," she replied, nestling herself securely against the shield of his much larger form.

"Can't we watch the sunset tomorrow?" whined their son out the car window, which promptly whirred closed making any reply his parents may have spoken null and void.

The rear window on the other side of the car came down.

"Muuuuhhm. Can't we just go? This is so boring." The higher pitch of their daughter's voice had the same tone of rampant *why would anyone want to stand around looking at a sunset over a rock?* disgust as her brother's. More of a stickler for answers, the window remained down for the whole ten seconds it took to realise neither parent was going to indulge her, then zoomed back up again; not before a few choice words found their way to her parents' ears.

***

The sun rose later in Australia's Red Centre than the family was used to living on the West coast, but by the time they arrived at the rock, the dry heat of the desert had already vaporised the morning condensation. The flies, after any moisture they could find, were impervious to any amount of shooing and flapping about of one's hands in the quest to remove them from facial cavities and scrunched up eye corners. Despite their frustration, the children were showing much more interest and enthusiasm for the planned activity than the previous evening. Climbing the vast, elephantine monolith was going to be far more exciting to them than watching the sun set over it.

The woman stood in awe. She would not climb the rock today. It was still too soon for her recovering adrenal system to deal with; being here with her family was enough. Taking in the sheer size of Uluru, she marvelled at how it came into being, heart and body simultaneously experiencing gratefulness and joy that she was here to marvel at it. Not so long ago she'd believed those feelings lost to her forever and a protracted unconscious unknowing was the only experience she had craved. Her greatest desire had been a freefall into dormant hibernation to escape the clutches of senseless isolation.

In recent years she'd maintained the physical appearance of the mother and wife her children and husband knew, but in all other ways had become unrecognizable: the result of a madman running her down with his car. Unable to locate a scrap of who she'd been in the months following, all hope that what was lost could be found had been annihilated.

She had soon learned that few had compassion for what they did not understand, and coming face to face with the eyes of her loved ones on a daily basis, full of disdain, had broken her further. What child could respect a mother prone to emotional meltdowns with no apparent cause? It hadn't mattered that she'd maintained a level of functionality that belied her internal chaos: getting up every morning, packing lunches, having dinner on the table each night. Small compensation for having to live with a stranger – irrational, emotional and crazy as fuck. What husband could love a woman like that?

A relief to all if she chose to go, she'd thought. Not depressed or suicidal, just tired, bone-weary, needing to find some way to smother the billions of sounds, smells, choices and decisions she had to face and endure every day. Disconnected yet overwhelmed; a terrible thing few could understand.

If a legal choice to end it all had been an option, she would have ironically viewed it as a lifeline – a welcome escape from an unbearable existence. But there had been no choice, and regardless of the pervading emotional disconnect, an inner voice reminded her daily that she loved her family too much to consider actioning any fantasy resulting in one of them finding her dead body in a bathtub filled with her lifeblood.

A smile tugged at the woman's mouth. After exploring the plethora of treatments available for PTSD, she had finally found one that had stuck and now, here she stood, almost whole again, in the shadow of a rock that felt no pain yet knew it well. The sound of her children chatting excitedly to their dad shifted her focus and she effortlessly joined the conversation. No longer a stranger, they willingly included her, sharing smiles that were real and radiating the connection she'd thought lost. Meeting her husband's eyes she was reassured of the promise he'd made to never again let her feel so alone.

How fortuitous, she thought, taking his hand, that she'd had no legal choice to lay down and drift away all those months ago.

MASTERS OF DISGUISE

Make-up on

Socialise

Constant jokes

Monopolise

Upbeat quotes

Energise

Facebook pokes

Fantasise

Perfect selfie

Criticise

Flawless body

Exercise

Smiling mouth

Empty eyes

Perfect lives

Suicides

Hypothesise

Question why

Despise their lies

You were hypnotised

By the Masters of Disguise

INSANITY

My mind, my thoughts; my reality

A minute, an hour; an eternity

My pain, your distress; our enemy

My decision, my choice; made carefully

Don't judge, don't question; my mentality

Just love, just accept; just hold me

Give me power, give me means; to leave grace-

fully

That I must ask is cruel insanity

WHY NOT?

It's true, I wish for death. I long for it as a child longs for another bowl of ice-cream and I feel the same sense of frustration, the same need to stamp my feet and shed hot tears when told no.

I am not depressed, yet twice a day I am given a mood stabiliser. It is placed in a tiny clear cup that is pressed to my lips by a nurse whose mouth is pulled into a tight grimace. She proceeds to dole out countless other tablets supposed to increase my comfort, but I suspect those watching on helplessly, benefit more.

If I press my lips together in an act of refusal, the Doctor comes and, with the patient voice and simple sentence structure one would use to explain basic concepts to a child, I am told why I must take them and what will happen if I don't. As if I haven't had that knowledge and fear scuttling around my brain for months.

That voice, those sentences, represent condescension in its worst form. Not old, I am made to exist in an aged care facility because there is nowhere else the motor neuron disease, creeping through the intricate web of my internal body, can best be managed; or so you tell me without quite meeting my gaze. You are good enough to try to shield me from your guilt and pity.

I am shrunken. Shrivelling physically, as my pain fleshes out. Soon I will no longer be able to swallow those tablets of comfort and the terrible symptoms of nerve cell degeneration will progress unimpeded. Everything that is going to happen to me because of this disease will happen regardless of what you do or what medications I swallow. Why prolong my agony? Why prolong yours? Why not let me go while it is still my choice, and before my dignity is left in the hands of others?

Why not now, before that pity and guilt I see in your eyes drowns out all the love I would much rather see?

Be it now or later, my pain and suffering will be felt to the end. The grief at my departure will cripple you no more than my staying. So why not now?

Why not gather around my bed, talk of all the events that made my life a beautiful experience. Make jokes, tell me all the things you'll do to fill your time once I'm gone and hold my hand, knowing as I drift away, your decision to make this about my right to choose, above all else, has granted me a final wish that only the compassion of a selfless love can grant. A peaceful death surrounded by the ones who have loved me most.

Would you not want the same?

SHAME

An insidious and undermining thing

Chokes my reality with tendrils sticky

Strangling and cutting off all joy

It seeks to stifle and destroy

To find its source is tricky

Toxic shame is its name

Repeatedly it's misread

Imprinted on me before my start

To sully, expunge and camouflage

What could be felt instead

IMPACT

Click, flick, comment, swipe

Data footprints stack and track

Sending thoughts, feelings, opinions

Across the world and back

Are cause and effect considered?

Does our conscience feel a tug

In rare mindful moments

Of which we are so smug?

Do we ever stop to wonder

If words or actions of our own

Have had meteoric effect

On a person or persons unknown?

Has an instinctive smile or gesture

Kept a stranger off a ledge

While impatient road rage

Sent another over the edge?

Is narcissistic satisfaction

Our heart-warming reward

As we share numerous opinions

From any vacant keyboard?

Did adding our two cents worth

To someone's end of day unwind

Set tomorrow's news in motion?

Does that ever cross our mind?

If the guy who shot his wife today

Was pushed across the line

By your response to a random comment

Would you be glad you took the time?

Sure you made it a week ago

From half a world away

A mindless reply to *friend* unknown

But it *ruined* someone's day!

We probably should remember

Words carry exponential power

Are open to interpretation

Can leave someone feeling sour

They can give a cause momentum

Be it for evil or for good

Heighten feelings beyond measure

Carry truth or great falsehood

What untold havoc

Has been unleashed today

From millions of human digits

Unthinkingly tapping away?

Ego driven behaviour

Not considered or thought out

Feelings too often shared

As quickly as they're felt

Hasty opinions, jokes, rebuttals

Slip from our fingertips

Read by someone unintended

'Cause our social account's public

Choose to neither take nor give offence

We're allowed to disagree

An alternative opinion

Need not be taken personally

We decide with every post

To relate or to react

Can choose positive experiences

For the *friends* our words impact

CLICHÉ

It's the age of non-judgement

Of not jumping to conclusions

Of labels given, unbidden

To foster tolerance and inclusion

Anxiety, depression, PTSD

Autism, psychosis, ADHD

Ethnic, indigenous, LGBT

Middle-age white guy, he, she

We tick boxes on forms

To create identity

To self-categorise

Trade-off singularity

We're not ticking boxes

To benefit from a label

The Man wants to store data

On our every meta detail

How do you identify?

What do you believe?

How much do you earn?

When were you conceived?

Data kept in a cloud

Un-hackable – what a con

Absolutely guaranteed?

Your privacy is GONE!

Labels interpret

Individual behaviour

Isolate, segregate

Food choice, sexuality, ethnic flavour

Baby boomer, millennial

Vegan, Muslim, straight

Come with cliché generalisations

Breeding right, wrong and hate

Don't buy into the fear

You need a label to succeed

Locked in chains of limitation

Your self-belief will seed

You'll find yourself deciding

What to wear and how to think

Based on opinions no more valid

Than your own innate instinct

Have labels stopped the judgement?

Is tolerance switched on?

Is acceptance mainstream?

Is the schoolyard bully gone?

We're complex individuals

Defined *not* by ink ticked box

It's no skin off my nose

Who you are or what you're not

We're 3D, unique,

Bringing more to the table

Than a self-fulfilling prophecy

Of a classifying label

You're not a cliché

Or a generalisation

You don't need singling out,

Fixing up or alteration

Your talents and dreams

The hopes hidden in your core

They're the real you

Perfection, not flaw

I'll be me, you be you

Put aside the clichés

You're not wrong, I'm not right

Assumption never pays

Be real, be seen

As the brave authentic you

Not as the cliché dictating

All you are, say and do

ALREADY ENOUGH

We are women; we don't need to roar

our power's not noisy, obnoxious or sexual

It's in our ability to conduct our business

With boundaries in-con-tro-vertible

No-one needs to see our boobs

Our arse or shapely legs

Sexualising our feminine

Makes us powerless instead

Relying on raising visual appeal

To gain approval and validation

An unwinnable game with judges fickle

What once was gorgeous becomes aberration

Our fearless female ancestors

Fought hard to win the vote

So we could use our voice, not our looks

To be heard amidst menfolk

But for all their fighting to raise our worth

Something's gone arse about

It would seem that more than ever before

Female assets are hanging out

I wish it was intelligence on show

Solidarity and cohesion

Instead, it's boobs, lips, bums and cheekbones

On 'Sex Sells,' we've called Open Season

We sexualise ourselves to distract

In case our minds don't measure up

Offended when not taken seriously

Who's responsible for this social construct?

Women need to own this one

Open our eyes and minds and see

We're responsible for this state of things

We've not owned all we can be

There is no conspiracy theory

Forcing us to be what we are not

There's no secret clan of men

With an illicit *Make Women Weak* plot

We are doing that all on our own

Selling ourselves way short

Thinking and acting like we've something to prove

We don't – that battle's been fought

We are women, we can roar

We can be loud, obnoxious and sexual

But our power lies in believing

We have inherently *all* that's essential

URBAN HAIKU

Eyes empty of hope

Look up at passers-by from

Bed on cold pavement

Empty city mall

Dawn announced by dove's call

Man stirs within box

A single tear slides

Unchecked to fall on table

Grief fills a moment

Urban mobile home

Secrets shame within its walls

Of flimsy cardboard

Music borne on wind

Lightens hearts along the mall

And pockets of coin

RETREAT

A shout out to fellow humans:

Who's feeling polarised and unstable?

Unsure of who they are or

If what they're feeling is relatable

Who's scared to attempt connection?

Who's completely unenthused

Unsure of what's PC

Mistrusting instincts too confused?

It seems the act of reaching out

Is now a big taboo

Everyone's looking for a platform

To compete and to outdo

We are equal plain and simple

But different none the less

With individual strengths

That put together could coalesce

Into something strong and beautiful

The polar opposite of weak

The epitome of tensile strength

Interdependence is what I seek

Why don't we collectively

Identify as humanity

Rid ourselves of the insanity

Of categorising our diversity

Which is creating such disparity

Loneliness and lack of clarity

It's just an idea.

Once we stop trivialising our place

We'll stop imagining others are too

We'll open up to receiving

With self-respect and gratitude

Not entertaining for a second

Interaction is anything but kindness

All this PC way of thinking

Has led to a certain type of blindness

The kind where we no longer

Seek to help another human

In case we cause offence

Life's all anxiety and confusion

We're offended when help's offered

Offended when it's not

Afraid to reach out

Afraid to cause insult

Afraid to ask a question

Called bigoted when we don't

Afraid to trust who we don't know

Called racist when we won't

Afraid of almost everything

We retreat retreat retreat

Not recognising the war

Will we recognise defeat?

Q AND NO A

I'm not sexist or racist, elitist or baby boomer

I'm not a uni grad, homophobic, gen y or x or zoomer

A computer is the only thing that asks if I'm robotic

What I truly am is bewildered by a country gone psy-

chotic

The fact that I must state these things before I even start

Indicates the rapid rate this place is falling apart

Why is junk food cheap yet it's cost on health, extreme?

Why is welfare on the rise and our homeless statistic ob-

scene?

Why is tax on ciggies huge, but small on sugar and fat?

Why is good food so expensive? Its medicine, that's a

fact

Why are kids of ten living on our streets

When we're the lucky nation, refugees flock to us in

fleets?

Why are we mining our resources and exporting them

still raw

For other nations to value-add and sell back at ten times

more?

Why are we not forging infrastructure that bestows

Intrinsic self-sufficiency on our nation as it grows?

Not value-adding to resources because we can't compete

Is short-sighted, destabilising and reeks of political de-

ceit

What about our oldies – the ones who made this country

great

Went to war, did it tough, always ready to help a mate

They're living it up in nursing homes, underfunded by

their pensions

Earned with fifty years of hard work, low pay and honest

intentions

Yeah, they're having a great time; most get to shower

every day

There's the odd bit of cruelty, but generally, it's okay

Don't blame the government, they're not paid to be long-

sighted

Three years is all they've got to fix what the previous

government blighted

How could they foresee there'd be no money to take care

of the aged

They couldn't possibly have known war on obesity

would have to be waged

Who knew sugar and fat, eaten in quantities huge

Would cause a health crisis of diabetes and a heart dis-

ease deluge?

Why are we selling our land and water to countries with no allegiance?

Why aren't we fighting to protect all our resources with expedience?

Why aren't we playing the long game to build a strong and healthy nation?

Why aren't we demanding the best for our deserving population?

Why are we settling for less than the great country we can be?

Why aren't we united by social outrage – instead of apathy?

DoILookLikeIGiveAFuck?

This is a call to arms

Not of the death and destruction kind

But to question everything you hear

Seize unbiased facts and arm your mind

Tick 'I'm not a robot'

With each transaction you make online

But you keep saying dilligaf and

Robot status? Just a matter of time

Was today's news pure fact

Or a biased reporter's version

To assert their opinion as truth

Via passive-aggressive coercion?

Did you share it at work?

With great conviction state it as fact?

Did your audience question its truth?

Did you shrug and reply 'Dilligaf'?

An online search for answers

Results in pop-ups sidetracking you

Co-incidentally targeted

Purposely distracting you from the truth

Convinced someone's watching?

Listening, recording all we do?

Not someone – a meta-data program

Building a profile of you

With all your shrugging and trusting

You gave the program permission

You skipped the fine print, ticked okay

Thinking *ahh what harm could it do?*

It's not 'Big Brother' watching

Good conspiracy theory I know

It's worse – profit-hungry corporations

Collecting saleable marketing info

Robots, we may not be

But we're programmable just the same

Curiosity; questioning all

Is how you keep your head in the game

Society's carved up

Collectives, segregated and grouped

A ploy to keep us busy fighting

Because united we couldn't be duped

Don't believe all you're fed

Without question or doubt

Swap out apathy, get invested

Stop dilligaffing about.

CHOOSE

WHEN THE RAWNESS OF DEEP EMOTION

HAS BEEN FELT

AND THE LAYERS OF FANTASY

STRIPPED AWAY

THERE IS NOTHING LEFT TO SEE BUT TRUTH-

NOTHING LEFT TO DO BUT CHOOSE

NOT YOUR FAULT

You've not failed in your care

It's not your fault I have to go

I had to do it this way

There's no softening the blow

Shed a tear, go ahead

One for me, two for you

More, for our choices

being decided by a few

I see you suffer at my suffering

It's exhausting, wears me thin

I no longer have the volume

to contain it, hold it in

My dignity is gone

Nappies, tubes I can't abide

I want you here with me

as I cross the great divide.

It's OK to end the suffering

of a well-loved family pet

Can't humane be applied to humans?

That's something I don't get

It's not your God-damned fault

I had to walk this path alone

Not your fault it isn't a choice

Governing powers yet condone

I wish you could bear witness

as peace steals across my brow

I refuse to be a victim

I choose power

I choose now.

BLURRED LINES

It's not like I chose this. I became a doctor to help people; to ease their suffering. I wanted to find cures for terrible ailments, see the smile on loved one's faces as their wife, son, uncle or grandmother was brought back to full health. But this? I'm out of my depth, sliding back and forth across my moral centreline like waves on a beach.

Looking at my patient, who I feel I know better than some of my friends, I remember her stories. In the seven years she has been a resident of this aged care home, she has told me of the years she spent working towards becoming a concert pianist. The pain of giving up that dream because she was born at a time when women didn't pursue careers, they got married. She became the accomplished wife of a powerhouse executive and travelled the world by his side; entertaining, schmoozing and behaving in the exemplary fashion expected of a woman in her position. In time she became a mother, learned to turn a blind eye to her husband's infidelities and continued to play the piano for her own enjoyment. She's lived a full life and her mind is just as sharp today as it has ever been.

My mind is not made up.

Medications alone are keeping this tired soul tethered to an existence that has shrunk, like her body, to just a tiny room. Possessions of a lifetime sold off, given away, shared among family. The piano she loved long gone, hands too shaky to hit the right keys and as her heartbeat flutters about in a similar fashion, my mind joins in. Thoughts, reasons to, reasons not to, jittery and confused, flap about like a trapped butterfly.

Kate watches from the side of the bed. Her mind, like her mother's, is made up. It is time to let go. I look at them both, meeting their gaze in turn and place the patch, that should be stuck to the skin covering this frail woman's heart, on the bedside table and take her hand. Gratitude erupts across her face and a sense of clarity settles over me.

Yes, I took an oath to do no harm – what that means anymore I sure as shit don't know, but my gut tells me this decision should be hers alone.

Experience. Time. Life. These things have blurred the lines.

SHADES OF GREY

I have known all the happiness, confidence, and self-assuredness a childhood stemming from love will bring. My parents were staunch Christians but favoured filling our home and lives with joy over fear and austerity. They kept the rules simple. Family is the most important thing. Nurture it, trust it, rely on it and meet every member of it where they are at, without judgement. God alone is all-seeing so the judging must be left to him.

My mother, a beautiful woman both inside and out, was diminutive in stature, outgrown by all five of her children before we reached our teens. Her presence, however, filled any space she occupied and oftentimes overflowed beyond it. It was a feeling enveloping each of us like a warm winter jacket that could not be taken off; a comfort we never sought to escape.

A patient, compassionate, and fair woman, known for her even temper, she was in no way a pushover or anyone's wallflower. She never needed to shout, bully, or cajole to make her feelings known and have her requirements met. Rarely flustered or concerned with complaints and protests issuing forth from our mouths over the usual arguments and small injustices felt by children, she kept things simple. The rules were Black and White; there was no need for her to overthink or tie herself in knots. If we engaged in fisticuffs it was of small interest to her who had started it or what it was about. Those involved were sent off to complete one of the many jobs about the farm. She would most often choose a job that required teamwork and took long enough for the wayward souls to unite over their common annoyance at their mother, but not so long or arduous that resentment set in.

Dad was always sent to check on our progress and if it was found lacking there would be no recriminations, just quietly spoken guidance until the work was done. In contrast to mother, he was tall and as far from diminutive as one could get, but he was gentle, and his presence felt just as keenly.

Our existence was uncomplicated, kept that way by our parents' shared ability to remain focused on creating the life they wanted. They were respected within our farming community and sought out when impartial advice was needed along with the reassurance that what had been discussed would never become the topic of gossip or public humiliation. Black and White. Let God do the judging when and how he sees fit.

The lessons of childhood have stayed with me. Seeing me through unexpected events and the challenges that I've witnessed so many others get bogged down in and become powerless from uncertainty. The rules have allowed me to live a fulfilled and happy life, love my family unconditionally and come through the trying times with grace.

Even when my son came home in his early twenties to tell his mother and me that he was a homosexual, the decision to continue loving him as we always had, despite the good Lord's instruction on the subject, was not something we had to break our hearts over. There was no need for emotional upheaval or concern about what others might think. Nothing needed to change. The boy is my son. Family is everything. We love and nurture it, meet each person where they are at and although a sin in the eyes of God, my son's sexual preference need not be judged by me. There was not one second that I felt I needed to do anything but continue to love my boy and anyone he brought into our home.

At fifty I have been told I have Alzheimer's. Taking one's own life is not a decision I ever thought I would have to make or would want to lay at God's feet but looking at it through a Black and White filter, the lines are clear to me. Family is the most important thing I have. I must nurture, protect and trust in it. I know the path this disease will take. It is long and holds all who know and love you in limbo. Life is a sacred thing, but does the beating of one's heart dictate life? Or the functioning of one's mind?

My wife is forty-nine. Still young. Still beautiful. Fierier than my mother but carries her beauty inside and out as she did. A woman in her prime, young enough to find happiness however and wherever she chooses, if not tied to an invalid.

My children, my greatest source of fulfilment, are just beginning to spread their wings. All the adventures of life lie before them. Restriction by the dead weight of a father who no longer recognises their faces will not be their reality.

The decision is easy. Black and White. Any day now a parcel will arrive containing the means for me to take my own life.

I have been honest with them all about my plans and in return, despite their devastation, they have promised to be guided by selfless compassion. They will love and nurture me in life until the day comes that love and nurture means it is time to let me go.

I am at peace with the sin of taking my own life, thanks to my mother, who, just before she passed, shared one more pearl of wisdom. She told me we can put our faith in God to judge fairly because knowing our hearts gives him the clarity to understand all the shades of Grey.

A PROPER JOB

I am genuinely proud of myself. This time, I have done a top-notch job, the best I have ever done. No-one will be able to fault my planning and execution this time. There'll be no *If you fail to plan, you plan to fail* sentiments bandied about, which will make for a pleasant change.

Ironic that so near completion I feel more upbeat than I have in... well... always.

Despite my exertion, I am damn cold. Cold and numb. Not the bone-chilling cold you feel with a bitter wind and an icy ground that freezes your feet, despite your thick socks and lined boots. It is the painful burning kind that even a roaring fire cannot thaw.

The numbness has surprised me. It is not that which stems from complete emotional disconnect. I have lived with that all my life – it is something else altogether.

It would have been nice to have someone here with me to acknowledge my efforts, my struggle and now my success, but it is not to be. Too many people who know nothing of struggle make the rules, whilst hardly any of us who must endure it stay long enough to change them.

The tub of hot water I'm soaking in is doing little to keep me warm, but I finally feel something rising through the numbness. It's relief. Pure, but short-lived as the last of my life spurts from my wrists severed and torn.

A proper job. Done. At Last.

RAW

Raw, like someone has taken a grater to the surface of my skin, is how I feel. Shredded: my totality an open wound with nothing all-encompassing enough to stem its weeping and allow healing to begin.

I am frozen, unable to enter the room I'd been eager to just moments ago.

I thought today would bring clarity. That scientific facts, analytical data and explanations, offered up by an expert with a uni degree, would trigger an ah-ha moment for my husband. That compassion, long overdue, would be reflected in his eyes and he would take action to ensure our home became my haven. I believed insight might startle him once he learned the only place I felt safe was my psychologist's office – horrify him even, once he worked out I had only one hour a fortnight with her. One hour a fortnight where my heart would settle, my breath would slow, and my body could rest from its hyper-vigilant state.

I imagined it would impact heavily on him to learn coming home was, for me, as terrifying as going out. Fantasies I invented in my mind this morning gave me hope enough to remain curbside as the 998 bus passed by.

I want to go into this room and be enfolded in an embrace that will ease the pain of too many lost years. Instead, I stand frozen, vomit rising in the back of my throat, disbelief laying wreckage to the foolish daydreams and I wish desperately to go back in time. Go back and stand under the shower for one extra minute or brush my teeth until the toothbrush vibrates, signalling the end of the three-minute cleaning time. If only I could do that, my ears would not have to bear witness to the words I am now hearing.

"Yeah well," his voice is full of contempt, "I don't really care how many medical facts and diagrams of the brain are thrown at me. A diagnosis of PTSD's a bit of a stretch. Your mum needs to realise other people have suffered far worse." There's a pause, then, "We've all got shit to do and she just needs to get on with things. I'm not interested in coddling her."

His words chill me to the bone. Adrenaline is pumping. Fear sweats out through my pores. Tears leak silently from my eyes. Confusion, devastation shreds my insides. If my psych's explanations haven't worked, what will? The question petrifies. How much longer can I manage this heartache? These people say they love me, yet refuse to validate my pain or offer comfort. I can't make sense of the contradiction. Do I stay? go? give up? step in front of that bus? Or do I excruciatingly white-knuckle it through the millions of serrated moments that must pass before I can go, flayed and tattered, to one more appoint-

ment, one more hour of reprieve with my psych?

All I know in this unbearable moment – raw, is how I

feel.

BOUNDARIES

Brought up with a set of rules

Was I

Put others first, self-sacrifice, from hard work

Don't shy

I believed if I practised what I'd been shown

A life of happiness for me would be known

That if I gave all of me

Led by example

The love I'd secure

Would be reward ample

That respect and kindness in return I'd receive

That's the rules as they were taught to me

Too late

I've come to recognise

Rules aren't boundaries

In anyone's eyes

Where you're coming from or going to

Boundaries, not rules, take care of you

My responsibility, not yours

To make them clear

To hold firm, not retreat

When you don't adhere

To not forgive and accept with such invalidating ease

For the sake of being liked; desperate to please

So instead of commanding

Your deepest respect

You see only my weakness

And that you reject

Time now for me, my boundaries to define

Respect for self; before others, the non-negotiable line

THE HUMANE THING

I awake to the comfort of Bob's warmth alongside me. His weight on the mattress has me pressed up against him in the downward dip, but I wouldn't have it any other way. We have each made it through another night. My eyes fill with the flashes of rainbow-coloured sunlight, refracted through the string of crystals I've hung at the window, flickering and ever-changing on the walls. Bob stirs. He will be greeted by a world as dark as the one he woke from, the creeping blindness of old age leaving him with only the memories of the dancing rainbows on our walls to think on – or not. It's hard to tell now where his thoughts take him. The blindness has left his eyes empty of all the emotions I could so easily have interpreted years ago, and the expected hip complaints of old age mean I can't identify what purpose fills his stride, when he manages to hobble about.

We're a fine old pair. Him with his failing body and I with cancer, first found on my liver, spreading rapidly through me like the suffocating root system of ivy.

"What will become of us?" I murmur into his neck, the wiry hair tickling my nose as the scent of him seeps in through my nostrils.

His answer is to roll slowly over, the pain a barely audible whimper puffing out from his chest, and bury his nose into my neck. My best friend. The love of my life. I hate to see him like this. A tired, pale shadow of his former self.

He barely moves from the bed these days, so it is my turn to roll over and swing my feet to the floor like a rusted old machine, joints fused, an engine without the power to get them moving quickly, smoothly. For days now I have brought food to Bob, positioning it so he can reach it easily if I'm not in the room, but he usually leaves it until I return and feed it to him a spoonful at a time.

"I'll be back in a moment darling," I say stroking his head, and his eyes close as if in assent.

Before I return with his food, I must call my son. He has promised to help with whatever we need. Today Bob must be bathed and then he needs to go for a check-up. Jack says he will drop by at eleven, which gives me enough time to shower and tend to the things that must be put to rights before we go.

***

I am grateful to have Jack's help getting Bob in and out of the car. The effort to get him washed before we left the house has made it clear to me that I won't be bringing my darling home. The love and friendship Bob and I have shared over the years goes beyond any that I have shared with other friends, but it does not sway me in my decision. If anything, my depth of love keeps me focused on what is about to be my final act of selflessness in the relationship.

A humane end is administered by Bob's vet, as legally as we can drink coffee, and I am thankful for that. I am comforted that, while Bob drifts free of his pain, I can stroke the soft hair of his canine head and hold him until the warmth leaves his body. The vet offers to take care of Bob's remains, but I ask for him to provide a box for us to take him home instead.

"I'll bury him for you now, mum," my son says kindly when we arrive home and he hugs me to him for a moment. I pull back so I can look at him when I answer.

"Not now son. I want to sit with him for a while. Would you mind terribly, coming back tomorrow?"

"Sure Mum. No probs at all. I'll just bring him inside, yeah?" I nod and he follows me in, placing the box containing Bob by the open fireplace in the lounge room.

"I'll make you a cup of tea," he offers, but I am impatient now for him to leave. My own painkillers are wearing off and I need to regroup before I can face the rest of the day's tasks.

"No, darling. I'm fine. Really. I just need to sit quietly for now." I squeeze his arm to reassure him and he leans in for a hug.

"Love you. Rest up OK? I'll be back tomorrow first thing to bury Bob." He gives me another squeeze. "You made the right choice, mum. I know it was hard, but he was ready to go, and it was the humane thing to do."

"I know, dear. Don't fuss. You get going. You've spent enough time on me today." I give him a small push towards the door, then watch him through the window as he drives away, mixed emotions sitting heavy in my chest.

There's only one more thing I need to do today. I wish wholeheartedly that Jack could sit by me and stroke my hair as I did Bob's just hours ago, but this is something I must do alone. Only I can offer myself a peaceful death and there's no need to wait, now that Bob has gone. I will lay down near my darling friend, drink the single dose of

pentobarbital I ordered some months ago, and drift away

from my pain as I run my fingers through his beautiful

hair one last time.

My son will understand. It's the humane thing to do.

EYES UP

Accusing me of being less than

does not make it true

It says nothing about me

more about you

Does it feel good

to wear me gossamer-thin?

To watch me shrink

and fade within?

Is this your understanding

of a sensitive love?

Or is destroying it more

what you're thinking of?

Your displeasure of me

appears rigid, unshakable

Loathing in your eyes

unguarded, unmistakable

Silence stretches gracelessly out across the day

I will never measure up

Head down, I walk away

Pain brings an epiphany

I finally understand

Your love for me is not a tangible thing

that I can ever command

My efforts must only

reinforce me

An agreement with self

to be all I can be

So, while with derision

you think to make me weak

My fighter within

is building her physique

One with a backbone

ready to play

Your mocking eyes miss that

as I walk away

I have a choice

I don't have to stay

I don't have to believe

or listen to what you say

Eyes up, I catch glimpses

of a destiny new

Head high, I can see

where I'm walking to.

HEART OF GLASS

You come and go like the wind

whenever you please

Sometimes a hurricane

Sometimes a gentle breeze

Bringing blustery moments

of warmth that caress

Ensuring love and trust

blossom in my chest

Then comes the ice

the bitter winter chill

Freezing me out

alone against my will

I shut down, hibernate

wait for winter to pass

Your leaning in announces spring

but my heart has turned to glass

A brittle fragile thing

that won't survive another blast

Of all that hot and cold

in unpredictable contrast

There's only so much pain

so many tiny hairline fractures

that can exist upon a heart

before it well and truly shatters

I wonder if you notice

Is my splintering on show?

Will you be taken unawares

when it comes my time to go?

ACCEPT

SOME DECISIONS ARE NOT OUR OWN

BEARING WITNESS CAN LEAVE US BEREFT

LOVE, COMPASSION AND ACCEPTANCE

ARE SOMETIMES ALL THAT'S LEFT

SMILE AT THE PARTY

"Mummy wants to die."

I freeze, teaspoon of sugar halfway to cup. My friend Kat, spares me one of her looks and replies to my son instead.

"Why does mummy want to die, poppet?"

His bottom lip trembles as his four-year-old eyes meet hers. "She hurts." He turns to me. "Don't you mummy?"

I smile, reaching for his chubby little hand.

"Yes, darling." My sentences mirror his: short, saying only what is required. Pain saps any energy for more. I choose not to numb the pain, determined my son will remember me awake and interactive. I will continue like this for as long as I can. Then, I will take my pill and go. His last memory of us together will be animated; full of love, smiles and happiness.

I refuse to take part in the days long process that sees me in hospital; my morphine slowly increased until I am more asleep than awake, my son passed into the care of friends while Jay and my sisters hold vigil by my bed until, finally, my heart stops.

I won't have my son wake one morning – after an unknown amount of time among adults behaving overly chipper to take his mind off his absent but not yet dead mother – to his father's haggard face that tells him he has lost what he didn't want to lose.

Thankfully, Jay agrees. I don't know if I can expect the same from Kat.

"Dead means I won't see her eva gen." My baby, all innocent but wise beyond his years, is focused on Kat.

"That's right, poppet," she answers, and I see the sheen of tears glistening, barely contained, in her kind hazel eyes.

My sweet boy moves in to comfort her. "It's k," he says, scrambling onto her lap and cupping her face with the hand I have just relinquished. "Mean pain, be dead too." He looks at me again. "Won't it mummy?"

"You got it, gorgeous," I reply.

"Then we have a party?"

I nod.

"A *see you later nasty pain* party," we say together before he turns back to Kat and asks, "Will you come, Kit Kat?"

Nodding, a wobbly smile on her face, she rubs her nose playfully against his. "I'll be there, Mr Bear."

"Good!" His face takes on a serious look. "But you're only 'lowed to smile at the party."

"Is that so?" Kat stares at me, arching an eyebrow; it's one of her looks.

"Yup, it's the rules. Gotta smile, smile, smile...."

"Cause mumma don't hurt no more," we finish together.

The front door slams. Jay is back, bearing shopping bags full of all the things I said I'd like to eat. There's a bottle of Riccadonia tucked under his arm. We'd drunk it at our wedding.

"Hope my darling wife and son haven't run you ragged," he jokes with Kat, planting a kiss on top of my head.

"The diva had me painting her toenails, of all things. Although, she generously informed me, I was the only one she could trust to do a good job," Kat replies.

"Oooh. Give us a look then, love." Jay peers down to my toes.

"Ahh, the old Peek a Boo Blue," he grins at Kat's raised eyebrow. "Wore it on our wedding day. Her absolute *fave of all time*," he explains using finger quotes.

"I'm impressed," says Kat. Then, "Right, well, much

as I'd like to stay," she tickles my son into hysterics as she speaks, "and think up new nicknames for this little pest," she smothers him with kisses, "I gotta go get ready for a party."

She's worked it out.

"Bye-bye, my darling diva." Leaning in for a hug, gentle against my fragile body, but potent with emotion strong enough to annihilate the heart, she whispers, "Love you to the moon and back."

"You too, Kit Kat," I reply, taking her hand as she draws away. Our eyes meet for the last time. "Remember to smile at the party."

"It's the rules," she replies.

And then she's gone, as I will be, come tomorrow.

ALL I NEEDED TO KNOW

The doorknob resists my efforts to turn it. I check for the spare key, which can usually be found in a crevice atop the door frame, and come up empty. Confirmation sits heavy in my gut.

The sirens can be heard within minutes of my call and I ready myself to perform the part I willingly agreed to play. I must trust she remembered to do everything we discussed as essential to the best possible outcome, before she removed the spare key and locked the door.

Neighbours peek from behind curtains when the police and ambulance park in the driveway.

"Have you been able to find a way in?" a policewoman asks, walking towards me.

I shake my head. "The key is gone."

"And there's been no answer to your knocking or shouting?"

Another shake of my head.

"You mentioned on the phone she is quite frail. Is it possible she's had a fall?"

This time I nod. The less I say the better.

"OK," as she rubs my arm, mistaking my silence for distress. "We'll find a way in. Don't you worry."

I know, without having checked, that the bedroom window will be slightly open. It won't be long until it's found, but has her impatience to get this thing done made her forget the most important detail?

The front door opens and a grim-faced police officer motions to the ambulance guys before making his way over to where his colleague and I stand.

"Are you related to the owner of this house?" he asks.

"My Aunt." I start to move forward, but he restrains me gently.

"You can't go in there. I'm so sorry, your Aunt is dead."

His gaze, full of genuine compassion, is blurred by the tears brimming in my eyes.

"Does your Aunt have any other family close by?"

I nod. It is no longer a choice not to speak; the tight lump in my throat makes it impossible.

"I'm going to need their names and contact details. A note with four names on it was in her hand."

"A note?" She'd remembered.

"I'm sorry," he says again. "It appears to be suicide."

"Suicide?" My voice is a whisper.

He nods.

I answer his question. "Three children, close by. I'm visiting from Tasmania." My voice falters. "I just popped out to get milk and her medicine." I point to my shopping bags sitting near the door that hadn't opened for me; its resistance telling me what she'd done, but protecting me from seeing it.

The note made clear to her children what I already knew – all I'd needed to know before agreeing to play a part that ensured it was not one of them that found her. The pain she'd been living with was inescapable, unbearable and, watching her loved ones watch her fade, an unacceptable option. My aunt had chosen to find peace now. Control over that was all she'd had left.

ENTIRELY PAINLESS

"Your final appointment is at three."

"OK." He nods. One word. One nod. Efficient.

"Sign here, here and here." He does. I watch, feeling nervous, and something else.

"Until then, please do as you wish." She doesn't recognize the irony. I do, and my inner tectonic plates threaten to shift, opening a huge abyss along their fault lines which will never close.

"Thank you." He stands and I follow as he walks away.

I'd asked him to include me. Told him I wanted to be here.

He said he would; if he decided to do it.

I love him so much. Have done since the moment we met. Love at first sight, first touch, it does exist and in this instance – a cliché I know – it knows no bounds.

"Tea?" he asks. It's his only choice of hot beverage.

"Yes, darling." My mouth is dry.

We sit in the café until ten minutes to three. I try for conversation; so much I want to say, but his own analysis of the situation is brutally flawless, even in my mind, so I choke it all down with my tea.

"Everything is in order. The procedure is entirely pain-less and…" The doctor pauses, seeing me stiffen and my eyes well up as he speaks. "…You can sit with him as long as you like." He ends gently to soften the blow.

It doesn't. Sitting and watching will be the most pain-ful thing I have ever done; ever will do, no doubt.

We are shown to a room looking out over the garden.

He lays back on the bed and drinks the water the nurse hands him. It looks so clean, benign, not hinting at its pur-pose.

Taking my hand and staring unflinchingly into my tear-filled eyes, he speaks the last words he ever will. "I love you, mum. Thank you."

"I love you too, son..." A sob breaks free of the widening fissure. "So much."

It is all there is time for; all that matters.

It is done, he is gone.

My heart is broken.

A chasm forever unfillable opens in my chest and the hot, liquid lava of my love, a mother's love, streams down my cheeks.

OKAY

"Go away!" I demand, rolling onto my side, putting my back to the door yet another bleeding-heart social worker has just come through.

"Not a good time, then?" he asks.

What the fuck? Is he taking the piss? His neutral tone makes it impossible to tell. My head whips back around and I see no sign of piss-taking on the face of the tall, well-built guy standing by my bed. In fact, he looks as comfortable in his tanned skin and casual clothes as a snake in the grass. If I was capable of feeling anything, I would be surprised. These types are usually pasty, balding – even the women – and so dull I can't tell one from another.

"I can come back later," he says. It's a statement, not a question.

Turning my head back to the window, I mumble, "Whatever," resigned to going through the process that a steadfast and uninventive system has laid out to deal with people like me. No point in fighting it; I learned that lesson some time ago. Someone is sent after every attempt to soothe, coddle, wheedle and convince me out of my suicidal state. They bounce into my room with a transparently fake sense of upbeat bonhomie and talk at me with varying degrees of interest and sincerity depending on how new to the gig they are.

'So, you want to die." Another statement.

Its bluntness shocks me into a half-sitting position so I can eye-ball him.

"No," I reply, sarcasm unmistakable. "I'm just entertaining myself." My words are an angry slap that fail to make him flinch, which pisses me right off. Fine, I'll sling some foul language his way. Opening my mouth to let fly with the *C* word, he cuts me short with a raised pointer finger.

"Wait a sec. I'll just go and grab a chair." And he walks out. What the-? Ordinarily, I can't get them to leave. They hang onto my every word, no matter how offensive, trying to analyse it, find hidden meanings or discover a key they can magically turn to fix me.

"You were about to say?" He's back, chair in hand, questioning me as though he never left. He sits, and with eyes the colour of honey (liquid gold, warm, but entirely void of the apology or pity I have come to expect) makes eye contact. Not a social worker then – they apologise for everything as though my state of mind is their fault.

"Cunt," I spit at him.

"As in, I am one?" He's unfazed. I'm confused.'So, what's the plan?" he asks, when I fail to reply.

"The plan for what?" As a rule, it is I who controls these conversations, but my powers to do so seem to have gone AWOL.

"The plan for your next attempt."

"Who the fuck are you?" My voice is pitchy.

"Shit. I totally forgot. I'm Stu." Again, no apology, not even an outstretched hand for me to ignore in a big fuck you gesture. "I take it you are going to keep trying until you succeed."

"Well, I do want to be dead."

"Yes," he replies. "I'm not sure why everyone's missed that. It seems obvious." I can't tell if he's being sarcastic or serious and it's beyond frustrating.

"Are you a fucking mental patient here?" I ask, ringing the bell for a nurse.

"No, but I can be a bit mental at times." The grin accompanying his words indicates he's quite pleased with his joke, but I'm not fucking laughing.

"Everything ok here?" A nurse pokes her head around the door. "Oh, hey Stu." She comes in, not waiting for my reply.

"Hi, Mel. Didn't know you were on today."

"Yeah. Serena's sick so I'm filling in."

"They told me at reception there's some gastro thing going around. Was told to *enter at own risk*." Stu is bantering with the woman as I watch on, incredulous. I'm suicidal and these two wackos are talking about gastro, for fuck's sake.

"I'll leave you to it, then." Mel retreats without acknowledging me and I am left with Strange Stu.

The usual protocol of *make the suicidal person feel like the world can't go on without them* has been replaced with *let's just get on with our lives and see what happens*. It's weirding me out, but with pseudo bravado and a sneer to intimidate God himself I ask, "What the fuck new therapy is this then?" knowing whatever he throws at me won't make a smidge of difference to how I feel.

"Did someone say you were getting new therapy?"

"No."

He shrugs. "So, how do you want to do it next time?"

I've had enough of this shit. The pissed-off kind of angry I usually feel has subbed off and *I'm totally fucking confused angry* has taken its place. "Why are you being such a wanker?"

Stu remains unreadable, sure of himself. Completely not like anyone who's ever come to see me before.

"I'm just here to find out how you want to do it next time."

"Why? So you can try and stop me?"

His brow furrows, "No. So I can help you. Has no-one discussed this with you before?" The question carries frustration, but I sense it's not aimed at me.

"Have you lost your fuck-ing mind? I'm not fucking around just to get some attention, you know. I. Want. To. Fuck – Ing DIE as soon as fuck-ing possible." My voice is hoarse with emotion; the years of practice to keep my tone as cold and detached as possible with these people now proving to be as ineffective as speaking English to a deaf Russian.

"Yes, I know." Stu's answer carries no note of fear or uncertainty. It's empty of judgement, bias or hint of his own feelings. "It seems clear to me that there's nothing you want to live for."

"Wow, did ya work that out all by yourself?" I ask, itching for a fight, though sadly he seems unwilling to oblige.

"You have no secret desire to achieve anything?

"No."

"So, if I said you could have anything, any life you want with no regard of what it would cost or how it could be made possible...?" He trails off, and I jump in.

"I would say I want to die. It's not that hard a concept, mate. I want to DIE. Do you get it or are you a fucking numpty?"

"No-one has ever offered to help you?"

Jesus, will nothing goad this guy into getting pissed? "I've had every kind of bullshit help known to man thrown at me, just not the kind I want."

"Well, that's hardly help then, is it?" His voice is quiet, but every word is clear and full of raw understanding.

Something inside me breaks – or is maybe restored. I'm astounded by the realisation I've finally been heard. So many *experts* have told me over the years that I'm sabotaging my recovery by rejecting the help on offer. I've been made to feel like the worst kind of arsehole; selfish and unappreciative of everyone's time and effort. But they've all missed the point – why would anyone be grateful for not being heard?

Tears roll down my face, the moisture a stranger to my cheeks. I was four the last time I cried. From then, ice-cold anger took their place.

Stu reaches for my hand and I don't consider pulling away. He's done what no-one else has.

"Nothing worse than not being heard, hey?"

I shake my head.

"If you really want to die, trying to talk you out of it is not the least bit helpful."

I dip my head in accord, a sense of peace stealing over me. I am with someone who has no interest in judging or fixing me; who's genuinely OK with taking me as I am.

"There are places in the world that recognise certain physical, psychological and emotional ailments as just cause for an assisted death."

"I have no money," I cut in.

"All your costs will be covered. Give me the nod and I can get the paperwork started."

"Yes." There is no hesitation in my answer.

"I'll get the forms."

As Stu heads for the door I am struck by his appearance. Something huge has shifted in my psyche. I have seen beauty in nothing for many years, but at this moment,

I am tempted to admit to myself that Stu is glowing with an aura that seems not quite of this world. I'm being ridiculous. Clearly, the tears have washed away my common sense.

Relaxing back into my pillows I realise, for the first time ever, that I have a purpose, something to look forward to. The sensation of my mouth curving up into a smile feels foreign, but not unpleasant, and I don't bother trying to hide it when Stu returns.

Guiding me through the paperwork, Stu indicates where I need to sign.

"Mel says you will be discharged tomorrow," he says when we are all done. "You can choose to be placed under my care or be assigned a social worker, who will keep you under suicide watch 24/7 until deemed you are no longer a threat to yourself."

"If I go with you?"

"Then you're free to go do whatever you like for five days."

"What's to stop me from trying again?" I'm surprised he would be allowed to just let me go home.

He shrugs. "Nothing."

"You're shitting me. There's no way anyone's going to let me leave the hospital and do what I please for five days without some do-gooder shadowing me." I speak with the conviction of someone who knows.

Stu shrugs again. "Nope. Not shitting you. If you leave the hospital with me, what happens after that is no-one else's concern. Think you can find something to do for five days?"

I don't think he is being ironic, but I can't tell. All I've done 24/7 for most of my adult life is fantasize, plan and attempt to take my own life. Escaping the watchful eyes of carers has added to the challenge. What the fuck *am* I going to do for five days?

"You'll work it out," Stu speaks quietly.

Great, now he's a bloody mind reader.

"I'll leave with you," I tell him.

"We'll go straight to a post office, get a passport photo taken, fill out the application and get it signed and then I can drop you anywhere you like." His approach to planning my death seems blasé and annoyance is sitting sourly in my gut. Crazy considering I'm finally getting what I want.

"Then?" I ask, pushing on with the conversation to reassure myself I am not involved in some candid camera stitch-up.

"I'll let you know flight details once everything is sorted and we'll meet up at the airport a few hours before the flight."

"Suicide isn't normally so simple," I say.

"Assisted death," Stu corrects me. "And things are always easier when you're heard."

Stu makes a lot of statements, which is kind of good. It's the first conversation I've had in forever that hasn't included the question *And how does that make you feel?* repeated verbatim. I've always answered it with various forms of *Isn't it fucking obvious?* depending on how creative I've felt at the time.

I'm suddenly over this discussion. Its oddness has worn me out. It's been a bit of a head fuck and I can feel questions I'm not equipped to answer rising uninvited into consciousness.

"That's it then?"

"Yep. Mel will call me tomorrow, to let me know when to pick you up." Stu's already heading to the door and throws a "See you then" over his shoulder, before he's gone and I'm left alone, impressed he hears subtext, as well as the obvious. A rare gift: most people hear only what they want.

I feel wrung out. A well-earned rest is on the cards and there's no immediate reason why I should put it off.

Stu had been at the airport for thirty minutes before he felt his phone vibrate in his pocket. Yanking it free, he swiped the screen to view the message.

Won't make it Stu. Made other plans for today.

Plans other than dying? Stu's reply.

Yep.

Perhaps some other day then.

Perhaps. But not today.

Stu pondered for a moment on what reply he should send, but before he could decide another message came through preceded by a thumb's up emoji.

Could you post me my passport? Might go travelling first.

Stu grinned. *Sure.*

Moments later, phone in back pocket, he was strolling casually to the exit.

Funny bunch, these humans, he thought as he drove away. They'd been given free choice, but their penchant for control had them making rules about almost everything, which tended to negate it. Their primal instinct was to survive, but ego had them always wanting what they couldn't have.

Sixteen times he'd intervened. To sixteen suffering souls he'd offered what they'd been told they couldn't have and shouldn't want. Fifteen of them discovered that, without suicide taking up all their thinking space, there were other things to do. Way more, in fact, than they could fit into the five days he gave them. They'd chosen to put death on the back burner for a while.

The sixteenth had been diagnosed with early-onset dementia and was never going to reconsider. She felt her life would soon cease to have purpose and that was no life at all.

Stu indulged himself with a few unbroken minutes of jaunty whistling as he drove to the nursing home on his list. It was one of the many things he enjoyed while in human form. Hope, an emotion not unique to planet Earth, filled him. These Beings did seem to need constant fine-tuning, but if their collective consciousness kept accelerating towards enlightenment, he knew – they would be OK.

HOMEWARD BOUND

Thumb reaches across palm

Seeking the comfort of a ring removed

Realisation thuds in pit of stomach

A clear and visceral sign

The dream of a life desired is over

Now the long walk home

Back to self – so long unknown

PIECES OF HUMANITY

All that has come and gone before

Events, emotions, conditions and more

Are passed on in some modality

To shape and frame in some capacity

An individual's experience of reality

Brutality, insanity, irrationality, morality

Spirituality, depravity, congeniality, profanity

Merged with vanity and formality

Create unseen commonality

Between locality and nationality

Dissimilarity now a triviality

Allows possibility for solidarity

With understanding and rationality

Hope becomes an actuality

Not such a great calamity

If we embrace with more than cordiality

These fragments of mortality

Innate, raw pieces of humanity

GRATITUDE

A book never comes into being without some serious hard work and input from the ones the universe sends to help and for that and those gorgeous souls I want to express my gratitude. I will try to keep it short, but the more I think on it the more my heart fills with love for the people who have believed in me, stuck by me, encouraged me, held me, comforted me, made me laugh and offered me the greatest gift of all – connection.

Thank you my darling friends. You know who you are. A rag tag bunch who collectively are the glue that makes sense of all the bits and pieces of my life. Some I have known my whole life, and some are only recent connections in the scheme of things, but I am so blessed to be able to say that each of you adds to me.

Thank you to Jennifer, of Daisy Lane Publishing. Publisher, Author, educator extraordinaire. From the outset, you had nothing to gain from connecting with me, yet you did and then you generously, freely and open-heartedly answered my many and varied questions, mentored me, encouraged me, passed my work to others so I could receive the gift of critical feedback and saw through the darkness of my stories and poems and recognised hope. I thought it would end there, but it didn't. You refused to limit yourself to only publishing the types of manuscripts you had published before and offered me my dream in the form of a contract attached to an email. That willingness to be flexible, to deviate, to allow, told me my manuscript had found the perfect home, and I will be eternally grateful.

Kelly Van-Nelson; Author, mother, managing director, innovator, educator, powerhouse – thank you. When you invited me to get up and read a couple of my poems at your book launch for Graffiti Lane, you had no idea that you had just given me permission to find out if an audience would like what I had to say. I didn't even know that that's what I had been waiting for. Your encouragement sowed a seed of self-belief which blossomed into the confidence to put myself and my work out there come what may. I suspect that wherever you go you plant those seeds and I for one am grateful that we crossed paths and got to share time and space when we did.

Claire, my editor, thank you. Fresh eyes were exactly what my manuscript needed, and you carefully and respectfully polished it to perfection.

Neshka, you have a huge heart, an artist's spirit, and a tireless ability to give. It was only ever going to be you who could create a cover for this book. Thank you.

I owe a huge thank you to the Katharine Susannah Prichard Writers Centre for giving me somewhere to go to write and meet other writers. Two weeks sequestered away in a cabin on the property after being awarded The Katharine Susannah Prichard Unpublished Author Fellowship, gave me the time and space to finish this manuscript. The generosity of the staff with their time and advice on all things writing, publishing and social media is something I will always be thankful for.

And finally, all the girls of the Writefree Women's Writing group. This group welcomed me in, encouraged me, entertained all my alter-ego's, and have been my writing family for over two years. They edit tirelessly, give wonderful critical feedback and advice and are always there to jolly or bully – depending on what's required – one out of the writing doldrums. This is a group of women you'd be sorry not to meet. Thank you, girls.

If you think you may need to talk to someone, or if you think someone you know may need to talk, please contact one of the following organisations.

Family and domestic violence support:

1800 Respect national helpline:

1800 737 732

Women's Crisis Line:

1800 811 811

Men's Referral Service:

1300 766 491

Lifeline (24 hour crisis line):

131 114

Relationships Australia:

1300 364 277

NSW Domestic Violence Line:

1800 656 463

Qld DV Connect Women's line:

1800 811 811

Vic Safe Steps crisis response line:

1800 015 188

ACT 24/7 Crisis Line:

(02) 6280 0900

Tas Family Violence Counselling and Support Service:

1800 608 122

SA Domestic Violence Crisis Line:

1800 800 098

WA Women's Domestic Violence 24h Helpline:

1800 007 339

NT Domestic violence helpline:

1800 737 732

Beyond Blue

1300 22 4636

About the Author

Skylar J Wynter is an author living in the Perth Hills. Winner of the Katharine Susannah Pritchard Writers Centre Unpublished Writer Fellowship 2020, she writes poetry, short stories, flash fiction and is working on her second book. Skylar occasionally performs her poetry at open mic events around Perth.

CPSIA information can be obtained
at www.ICGtesting.com
Printed in the USA
LVHW021610250920
667128LV00011B/806